100
TRICKS TO
APPEAR
SMART
IN MEETINGS

FOR MY FAMILY, FRIENDS, COLLEAGUES AND,

ESPECIALLY, THE ONE WHO BECAME ALL THREE.

100
TRICKS TO
APPEAR
SMART
IN MEETINGS

HOW TO GET BY
WITHOUT EVEN TRYING

SARAH COOPER ☺ THECOOPERREVIEW.COM

◻ SQUARE PEG

TODAY'S AGENDA

PART THREE: NEXT STEPS **111**

FOLLOW-UP **159**

LET ME TELL YOU
WHAT I'M GOING TO TELL YOU
BEFORE I TELL YOU AGAIN

Like everyone, appearing smart in meetings is my top priority. Sometimes this can be difficult if you start daydreaming about your next vacation, your next nap, or bacon. When this happens, it's good to have some fallback tricks to fall back on. This book will give you 100 fallback tricks to fall back on.

By learning, internalising, and actionising all of the strategies here, you'll be well on your way to becoming a major player at your company without even knowing what that means.

Can I ask you a quick question?

Do you attend meetings?

Do you want to get ahead in your career?

Do you enjoy answering pointless rhetorical questions?

Did you buy this book for you or for someone else?

Then this book is for you. Or for someone else.

WHY MEETINGS? SERIOUSLY, WHY?

There are a number of reasons. We go to meetings to 'collaborate,' share 'information,' prove to everyone our 'job' isn't 'useless,' and mostly because we couldn't come up with a good excuse in time.

It's estimated that we spend 75 per cent of our waking lives in meetings, holding 11 million of them annually. But more than a third of those meetings are spent planning another meeting, while another sixth are spent asking someone to repeat what she just said because I wasn't paying attention, while still another three-sixths really should have been an e-mail.

No one pays attention in meetings. So, to get ahead, you need to not pay attention *better than everyone else*. The fact is meetings are one of the few opportunities you have to show your leadership potential, soft skills, and analytical creative thinking brain abilities.

The smarter you appear, the more meetings you'll be invited to, the more opportunities you'll have to appear smart, and the sooner you'll be spinning in a chair while staring at the ceiling and whistling, like the CEO always does.

WHERE DID THIS BOOK COME FROM?

I wrote this book because someone paid me to. But I also wrote it because I had a deadline.

I began jotting down meeting tricks in the summer of 2007 while working for Yahoo!, as I observed them first-hand in meetings with Directors, VPs, Senior VPs, and Senior VP Directors. Seven years later I became a manager at Google and got invited to even more meetings than I ever had before. How did I achieve such an intense trajectory over the course of my luminous career? I went to meetings, and I looked damn smart in them.

TIME SPENT IN MEETINGS

Source: TheCooperReview.com

Awkward silence

Awkward speaking over each other

Agreeing to anything just so we can leave

Staring at phone

Planning another meeting

Asking if you can repeat that because I wasn't paying attention

Realising this could have been an e-mail

WHAT'S IN THIS BOOK?

I'll be diving deep, deeper than any deep dive you could imagine, into every kind of meeting, from one-on-ones to presentations, showing you simple ways to nail your meeting game no matter what the situation. Then we'll sync up on how you can look like you're syncing up outside your normal work environment and even what to do when you're not in a meeting. And we won't skip the thorny, complicated mechanics – like what to do with your face.

This book will give you the tactics, methods, and other synonyms for 'strategy' that you need to push your career beyond your wildest dreams but without ever having to apply yourself.

TO CLOSE WITH A MOTIVATIONAL SUMMARY

Perception is reality. I believe it was Christopher Columbus who said that. And he was right. I've poured everything I pretend to know into these pages, and I sincerely hope these tricks do for your career what they did for mine.*

* I am now on permanent hiatus.

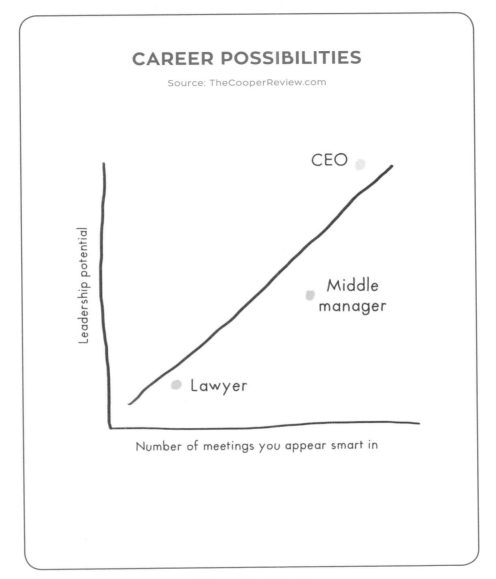

HOW TO READ THIS BOOK

- ☐ Buy this book
- ☐ Buy this book for all your colleagues (the ones you like)
- ☐ Schedule a meeting to discuss this book
- ☐ Schedule a follow-up meeting for no particular reason
- ☐ Keep a copy at your desk
- ☐ Keep a copy in all conference rooms
- ☐ Keep a copy in your suitcase for business trips
- ☐ Keep a copy on your bedside table as a coaster for your iPhone

PART
ONE

SETTING THE STAGE

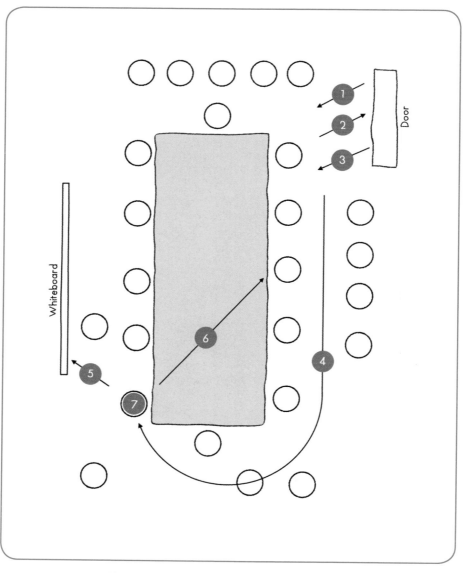

ENTERING THE ROOM

During meetings, where you sit, stand, lean, or crouch may mean the difference between being perceived as a future director or a future managing director. Follow this sample play-by-play to enter the room literally reeking of intelligence.

1. Enter the room; ask if anyone needs anything. (See Trick #61)

2. Leave the room, get some coffee, go to the bathroom, take your time.

3. Return bringing water and snacks, even if no one asked for any.

4. Sit near the meeting leader, so it looks like you're co-running the meeting. (See Trick #33)

5. Write a few key words up on the whiteboard. (See Whiteboard Tactics)

6. Make eye contact with your nemesis.

7. Lean back and look up at the ceiling while clasping your hands behind your head, as if you're deeply considering something.

GENERAL
MEETINGS

10 KEY STRATEGIES
FOR APPEARING SMART

General meetings generally fall into one of three categories: painful, useless, or soul-crushing. But no matter which of these types of meetings you find yourself in, you can be sure that one of these 10 tricks will make you appear smart.

#1 Draw a Venn diagram

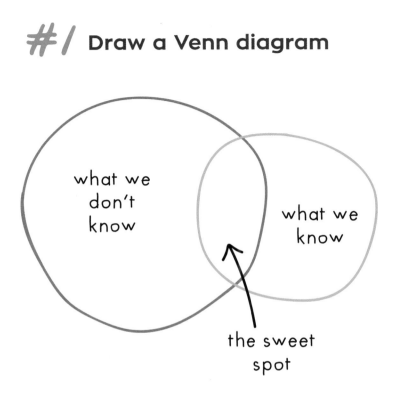

what we don't know

what we know

the sweet spot

Getting up and drawing a Venn diagram is a great way to appear smart. It doesn't matter if your Venn diagram is wildly inaccurate; in fact, the more inaccurate, the better. Even before you've put that marker down, your colleagues will begin fighting about what the labels should be and how big the circles should be. At this point, you can slink back to your chair and go back to playing Candy Crush.

#2 Translate percentage metrics into fractions

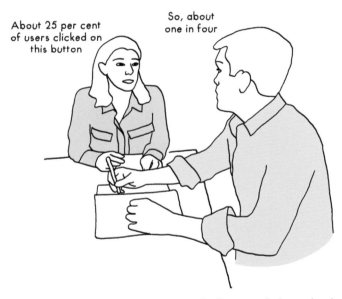

If someone says, 'About 25 per cent of all users click on this button,' jump in with, 'So about one in four,' and make a note of it. Everyone will nod their heads in agreement, secretly impressed and envious of your quick maths skills.

#3 Encourage everyone to 'take a step back'

Can we take a step back here?

There comes a point in most meetings where everyone is chiming in, except you. This is a great point to go, 'Guys, guys, guys, can we take a step back here?' Everyone will turn their heads toward you, amazed at your ability to silence the fray. Follow it up with a quick, 'What problem are we really trying to solve?' and, boom! You've bought yourself another hour of looking smart.

#4 Nod continuously while pretending to take notes

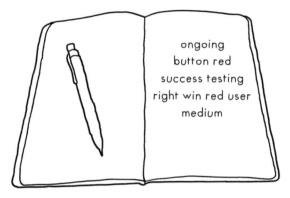

ongoing
button red
success testing
right win red user
medium

Always bring a notepad with you. Your rejection of technology will be revered. Take notes by simply writing down one word from every sentence that you hear. Nod continuously while doing so. If someone asks you if you're taking notes, quickly say that these are your personal notes and that someone else should really be keeping a record of the meeting.

#5 Repeat the last thing the software engineer said but very, very slowly

Make a mental note of the software engineer in the room. Remember his name. He'll be quiet throughout most of the meeting, but when his moment comes, everything out of his mouth will spring from a place of unknowable brilliance. After he utters these divine words, follow up with, 'Let me just repeat that,' and repeat exactly what he just said, but very, very slowly. Now, people will look back on the meeting and mistakenly attribute the intelligent statement to you.

#6 Ask 'Will this scale?' no matter what it is

But will it scale?

It's important to find out whether things will scale no matter what it is you're discussing. No one even really knows what that means, but it's a good catch-all question that generally applies and drives software engineers nuts.

#7 Pace around the room

Whenever someone gets up from the table and walks around, don't you immediately respect him? I know I do. It takes a lot of guts, but once you do it, you immediately appear smart. Walk around. Go to the corner and lean against the wall. Take a deep, contemplative sigh. Trust me, everyone will be shitting their pants wondering what you're thinking. If only they knew (bacon).

#8 Ask the presenter to go back a slide

Sorry, can you go back a slide?

'Sorry, could you go back a slide?' They're the seven words no presenter wants to hear. It doesn't matter where in the presentation you shout this out; it'll immediately make you look like you're paying closer attention than everyone else is, because clearly they missed the thing that you're about to brilliantly point out. Don't have anything to point out? Just stare silently for several seconds, then say, 'OK, let's move on.'

#9 Step out for an important phone call

Sorry, I have to take this...

You're probably afraid to step out of the room because you fear people will think you aren't making the meeting a priority. Interestingly, however, if you step out of a meeting for an 'important' phone call, they'll all realise just how busy and important you are. They'll say, 'Wow, this meeting is important, so if he has something even more important than this, well, we better not bother him.'

#10 Make fun of yourself

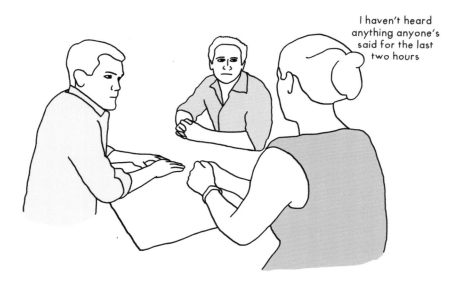

If someone asks what you think and you honestly didn't hear a single word anyone said for the last hour, just say, 'I honestly didn't hear a single word anyone said for the last hour.' People love self-deprecating humour. Say things like, 'Maybe we can just use the lawyers from my divorce,' or 'God, I wish I was dead.' They'll laugh, value your honesty, consider contacting HR, but, most importantly, think you're the smartest-looking person in the room.

WHITEBOARD
TACTICS

21 MEANINGLESS
DIAGRAMS YOU CAN DRAW

It can be incredibly intimidating to go up to the whiteboard and draw something during a meeting – everyone is glued to their seats in anxiety-ridden fear of moving. And that's precisely why it's one of the easiest things you can do to appear smart. Simply being up there increases your perceived leadership potential by a thousand per cent. But what should you draw? It doesn't matter. You could get up there and draw a bunch of arrows pointing to your butt and you'd still seem pretty darn smart. But if you want some more ideas, try one of these meaningless diagrams.

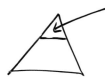

1. Write the word 'vision' with a circle around it. Remind everyone that everything we do must revolve around our vision.

2. Draw a triangle and an arrow pointing to it. Ask, 'Are we focusing on the right things?'

3. Draw a weird-looking bucket and call it a funnel. Say, 'We need to determine the best path for optimum customer acquisition.'

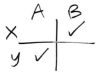

MILESTONES

Now   LAUNCH

4. Draw a horizontal line and then a vertical line right through it. Add some letters or checkmarks. Ask if we're meeting all our requirements.

5. Draw a bunch of boxes connected by lines. Big boxes at the top are important people, and small boxes at the bottom aren't. Ask, 'What's the hierarchy we're trying to establish?' and you'll look like a big box.

6. Draw a line from now to launch, with dashes that represent milestones. This will make people think you know how project plans work.

BACKEND
↓
FRONTEND

7. Write 'backend' and 'frontend' with an arrow connecting them. Say we just need to hook up the backend to the frontend. You'll seem very technical.

8. Draw a pizza with a question mark inside it. Say each project has different pieces and we need to find out which are the big pieces and which are the small pieces.

9. Draw an X- and Y-axis, then draw a line that looks like a hockey stick line. Circle the elbow in the hockey stick and ask, what's going to get us to hockey stick growth? What's going to move the needle 10x?

STRATEGY

DATA

10. Write words, such as 'strategy,' 'goal,' or 'action plan,' in big letters and with a double underline. Then just sit down. Your team will know you mean business.

11. Draw a few stick figures and say we need to talk about our customers. Circle one of them and say, 'This is Lucy. Lucy's a Mum. What does Lucy want? Who cares. What do we want? That's a trick. What does Lucy want?'

12. Draw a bunch of circles and some random things like 'money,' 'data,' or 'hot dogs.' Connect each thing with some lines and ask everyone if we can just connect the dots here, like you just did.

13. Draw a line with two arrows on either end. Walk to one end and say one word, then walk to the other end and say the opposite of that word. Then ask the team where they think we should be.

14. Draw a box with an arrow pointing outside the box. Say we don't want to be inside the box.

15. Draw a cloud. Say, 'Let's talk blue sky,' or ask, 'What about the cloud?' Either one will make you seem like a key driver of innovation.

16. Write the word 'roadmap' with a square around it. Ask your colleagues, 'What's our roadmap?' This will make it seem like you care about accomplishing goals.

A | B | C

17. Draw three columns labelled A, B, and C. Ask the team to separate our discussion into streams of thought. Then sit back down and let someone else do it.

18. Write the word 'ideas' with a squiggly line around it. This shows you really want to hear ideas, while the squiggly line shows how organic your process is.

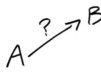

19. Draw a line with A on one end and B on the other. Ask, 'What will get us from point A to point B?' Your colleagues will appreciate you simplifying the solution like this.

20. Draw a 1, 2, 3 with arrows between them. Ask about each step we need to take and what those steps are. Then just write whatever people throw out there.

21. Draw a triangle with question marks at each angle. Say that any great strategy has three strong cornerstones. Ask, 'What are our cornerstones?'

HOW TO CONVINCE YOUR COLLEAGUE YOU CARE

The other day, my colleague confided in me about how he was feeling or something. To be honest I have no idea what he was talking about. The point is, listening to your colleagues is hard. And if you're the only other person in the room, your ability to seem fully committed, deeply engaged, and knowledgeable beyond anyone's wildest expectations will be under a microscope.

Here are 10 tricks to gain the respect of your colleague while simultaneously making sure he never realises how little you want to be in this room with him right now.

#11 Send a last-minute instant message asking if the meeting is still necessary

Send a message to your colleague right before the meeting and ask if the meeting is still necessary. Say you want to be cognizant of each other's time and make sure there isn't something more valuable you could both be doing for the company. Your colleague will be impressed by how much you respect her time. She'll also likely cancel the meeting to avoid the burden of coming up with something important to discuss, leaving you with an afternoon free to leave lengthy comments on random YouTube videos.

#12 Say you're just wrapping something up

Just give me two seconds...

Get to the meeting early and start reading your e-mails. When your colleague arrives, he'll get the sense that he's coming into your office. After greeting him warmly, say you're just wrapping something up and ask him to wait a minute. For extra points, ask him to wait outside the room. This puts you in a position of power over your colleague that he'll likely be unable to overcome, no matter what he throws at you.

#13 Say you don't have an agenda

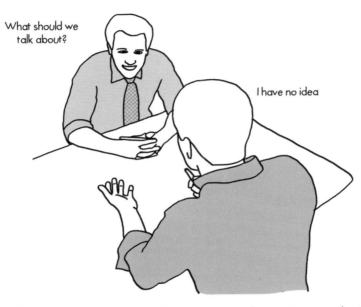

For weekly meetings, put your colleague at ease by saying you don't have anything in particular to talk about. Not having an agenda makes you seem friendly and approachable. Then, put the pressure on him to come up with something to talk about and get annoyed if he doesn't have anything. Suggest ending early. If this has happened more than a few weeks in a row, suggest cancelling the meeting altogether.

#14 React to everything as if you already knew that

Right, sure, of course

React to what your colleague is saying as if everything he's saying is pretty obvious. Cut him off with phrases like, 'right,' 'sure,' 'right, of course,' 'well, everyone knows that,' or 'duh.'

#/5 Suggest a 'walking' meeting

If your colleague wants to chat with you, it's always great to suggest a 'walking' meeting. Say you enjoy walking meetings because they clear your mind, just like they did for Steve Jobs.

#16 When your colleague brings up an issue, ask for an example

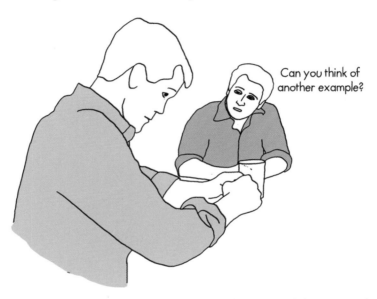

Can you think of another example?

When your colleague brings up an issue he's having, ask for a specific example. Then ask for a more specific example. Then say you really need more than one example to establish a pattern. Then suggest discussing it next time, when he has more examples.

WHAT ARE WE DOING IN ONE-ON-ONES?

Source: TheCooperReview.com

12% Praying our colleague doesn't cry

20% Trying not to cry

30% Crying

90% Pretending to care

96% Trying to end 15 minutes early

52% Talking about the weather

63% Hating that people always talk about the weather

92% Trash talking other colleagues

16% Dreaming of a career where you get to 'work with your hands'

#17 Make an obvious statement that can't be refuted

Getting your colleague to agree with everything you say is a great way to appear smart. And the best way to do that is to say something he really can't disagree with. Some great statements are:

- It is what it is.
- We need to be smart about this.
- We should focus on the priorities.
- We have to choose the right choices.
- Let's deal only in facts and opinions.

#18 Say everything you discuss is confidential

I really shouldn't be telling you this...

Ask your colleague to keep everything you say confidential, even if it's all common knowledge. This will make everything you say seem extra important. It will also make it more likely for your colleague to share something with you that she shouldn't, which you can use against her later.

#19 Share an 'objective' opinion

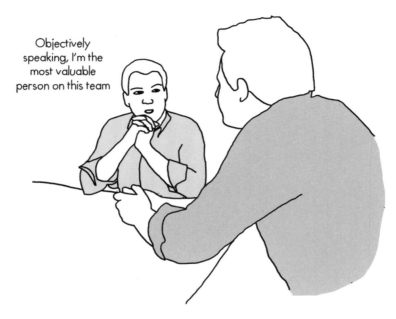

Objectively speaking, I'm the most valuable person on this team

All opinions are subjective, except the ones you explicitly label as objective. If you start a sentence with, 'Objectively speaking,' anything you say afterward must be a hundred per cent correct in every context and all circumstances no matter what your colleague thinks. Objectively speaking, this is how you should start all your sentences.

#20 Have a meta-conversation about the meeting

Be very concerned about making sure the meeting was helpful, useful, and helpful. Ask how the meeting could be better, then say you'll try that for next time but then don't.

EMOTIONAL
INTELLIGENCE
PLAN

WHAT TO DO
WITH YOUR FACE

It's important to make faces in your meeting. Making the right face at the right time will set you apart and create the illusion that you actually understand what's being discussed.

But sometimes it's hard to come up with the right face to make or new faces to make that you haven't already made hundreds of times. If you find yourself in that situation, try one of these faces.

1. Furrow your brow and tilt your head. This face says, 'That idea sounds familiar. Oh, yeah, because you stole it from our competitor.'

2. Point your chin down and purse your lips. This face says, 'I love it when you tell me how to do my job.'

3. Raise your eyebrows and smile. This face says, 'Someone brought cupcakes??'

4. Look tired. This face says, 'Who the hell keeps scheduling meetings for 8 a.m.?'

5. Squint your eyes and frown slightly. This face says, 'Did you just offer me plain tap water?'

6. Smile slyly. This face says, 'Yes, I am still working on that.'

7. Close your eyes. This face says, 'I'm listening very intently, I swear.'

8. Put your chin on your fist. This face says, 'That's an interesting perspective, Nathan; tell me more.'

9. Raise your eyebrows and point. This face says, 'Oh, right! We did forget to document that decision.'

10. Smile widely. This face says, 'Great speech, boss.'

11. Look excited. This face says, 'Hey! Almost beer thirty!'

12. Smile and turn your head to the side. This face says, 'Didn't I see you at the gym last night?'

13. Get a blank look on your face. This says, 'Worst. Idea. Ever.'

14. Look around the room. This face says, 'Is anyone writing this down?'

15. Furrow your brow and smile. This face says, 'Schedule *another* meeting to discuss this? Sure.'

16. Scrunch your nose. This face says, 'Was that a fart?'

17. Recoil with fear. This face says, 'You just wrote on the whiteboard with a permanent marker.'

18. Take an air of superiority. This face says, 'My mere presence adds value to this meeting.'

19. Look up and to the side. This face says, 'Hmm, I don't remember saying I'd do that.'

20. Take a bite of your salad. This face says, 'I just took a bite of salad so no one can ask me anything.'

21. Get a sheepish look on your face. This says, 'Yes, we've been talking about streamlining this process for 18 months now.'

CONFERENCE
CALLS

HOW TO SOUND SMART
OVER THE PHONE

When you dial into a meeting from somewhere else, it's actually really hard for people to tell you've spent the last half hour looking at pictures of your cousin's dog on Facebook. In fact, I'm writing this on a conference call right now, and, yes, I still sound like the smartest person in the room. Why? Because of these 12 tricks.

#2/ Ask if everyone's here

Before the meeting starts, ask if everyone's here. You might even pick out a specific person and ask if she's here, and, if not, ask if she is supposed to be here. Not only will your colleagues appreciate your diligence but also you'll seem like a real people person.

#22 Talk about the weather and/or time zone where you are

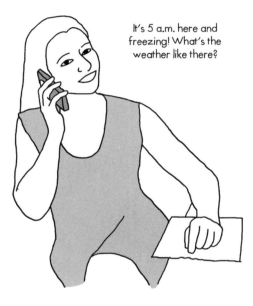

It's 5 a.m. here and freezing! What's the weather like there?

Let everyone know where you're dialling in from, and mention the weather and ask what the weather is like where everyone else is. Talk about what time it is where you are, especially if it's any part of the world where the fact that you're even awake is truly amazing. Your dedication to the company will be wildly apparent, but best of all everyone will know not to expect your full participation.

#23 Ask everyone who isn't talking to put themselves on mute

Could you mute yourself, please?

Everyone hates background noise, but only true business leaders have the guts to get rid of it. Interrupt whoever is talking and ask, 'Where's that noise coming from?' Follow up with, 'If you're not speaking right now, could you please mute yourself?' Now the call will be smoother and quieter due in no small part to your executive leadership skills.

#24 Stop the meeting to pull up the data

Let's pause for a second
while I pull up that chart

Stop the conversation so you can pull up the data, and remind everyone we should be making data-driven decisions. Ask if everyone else is looking at the data, too. Once everyone has confirmed, say, 'OK, we can go ahead now,' then go back to reading sports or celebrity news.

#25 Ask 'Who's speaking?'

If someone starts talking without announcing who she is, interrupt and ask, 'Who's speaking?' even if you know who it is. This is a great trick to use when you know you probably won't say anything else on the call.

#26 Take the call using some 'cutting-edge' technology

I'm joining you from the future

Announce that you're joining the meeting using your new smartwatch or some other cutting-edge technology. Your colleagues will always be impressed that you're trying new things because they'll think it means you know more than they do about the future. Apologise in advance if your call is dropped due to your gamechanging experimentation.

#27 When someone mentions a large number, put it in terms of a city or country

25,000 customers? That's like the size of a small village in Saskatchewan

When someone mentions a large number, put it in terms of a city, country, or other geographic location. If you don't have one handy, just make up some population of people. Your colleagues will be impressed by your deep knowledge of the world census.

#28 Say 'That's exciting' or 'That makes sense' or 'Very cool'

Thanks for that.
Excellent insight.
Very exciting.
Cool.

Since no one can see you nodding or smiling throughout the meeting, it's important to interject at least once every two minutes so that people know you're there and you're totally following everything being said, even though you're really playing Sudoku.

Some great phrases to use are: 'Thanks for that insight,' 'Yeah, totally,' 'Going to have to think about that some more,' 'Interesting,' 'Wow,' or 'Hmm.'

#29 Instant message other attendees during the call

Send quick instant messages to others during the meeting, such as, 'Is this making sense to you?' 'What are your thoughts on this?' and 'My lunch today was the bomb dot com.' Your colleagues will be impressed by your multitasking skills.

#30 Suggest taking that offline

When you have no clue what anyone is talking about, suggest taking that offline. Remind everyone that deep discussions are better in person. When someone asks what constitutes a deep discussion, say you're not sure, but you're open to discussing it (offline).

#3/ Make sure everyone is looking at the latest version of the document

I'm looking at the version with red headers. Does everyone see the red headers?

When reviewing a document, interrupt to say, 'I know this has gone through a few revisions; I just want to make sure we're all looking at the latest one.' Everyone will scramble to figure out how to verify that everyone's looking at the same thing and thank you for pointing that out.

#32 When someone asks if we've covered everything, say, 'I had a few thoughts, but I'll save them for e-mail'

I'll follow up later

It's the end of the call, and the organiser wants to make sure we covered everything. This is a good time to say you still have a few things to cover, but you'll discuss them separately. This makes you seem like you're saving everyone's time and no one will remember to follow up on your follow-up anyway.

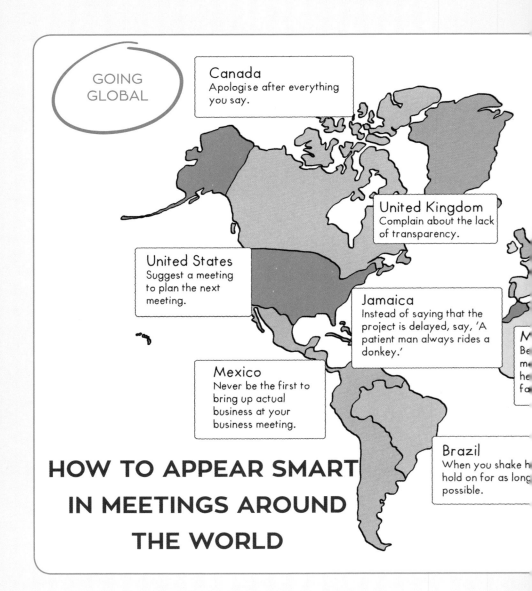

GOING GLOBAL

Canada
Apologise after everything you say.

United Kingdom
Complain about the lack of transparency.

United States
Suggest a meeting to plan the next meeting.

Jamaica
Instead of saying that the project is delayed, say, 'A patient man always rides a donkey.'

Mexico
Never be the first to bring up actual business at your business meeting.

Brazil
When you shake h
hold on for as long
possible.

M
Be
me
he
fa

HOW TO APPEAR SMART IN MEETINGS AROUND THE WORLD

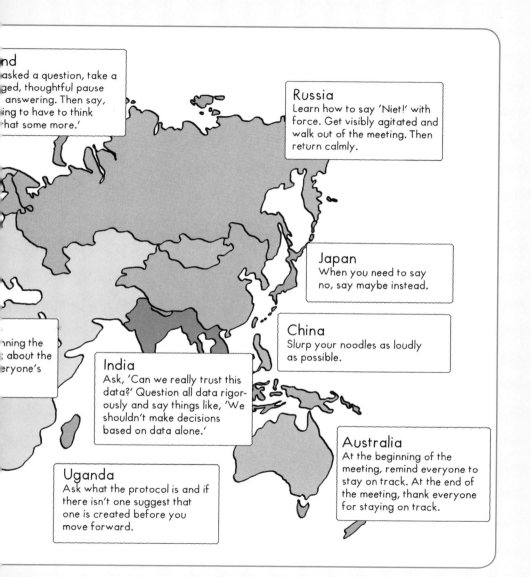

nd
...asked a question, take a
...ged, thoughtful pause
...answering. Then say,
...ing to have to think
...hat some more.'

Russia
Learn how to say 'Niet!' with
force. Get visibly agitated and
walk out of the meeting. Then
return calmly.

Japan
When you need to say
no, say maybe instead.

China
Slurp your noodles as loudly
as possible.

...nning the
...about the
...eryone's

India
Ask, 'Can we really trust this
data?' Question all data rigor-
ously and say things like, 'We
shouldn't make decisions
based on data alone.'

Australia
At the beginning of the
meeting, remind everyone to
stay on track. At the end of
the meeting, thank everyone
for staying on track.

Uganda
Ask what the protocol is and if
there isn't one suggest that
one is created before you
move forward.

PART
TWO

CORE CONVERSATION

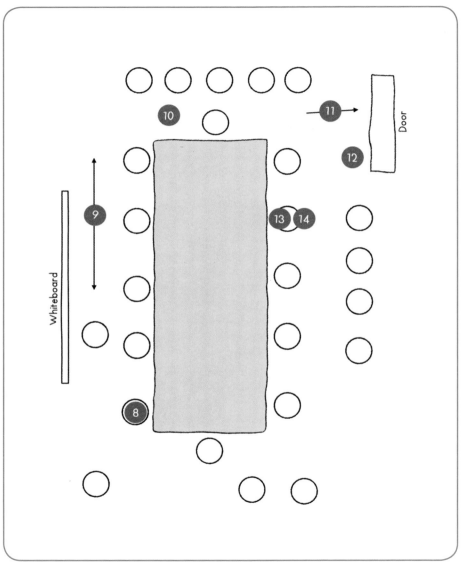

OWNING THE ROOM

During the meat of the meeting, it's easy to lose focus and fall apart. Here's how to weave a few tricks into your meeting performance so that no one knows you stopped paying attention before you even got there.

8. Take a bite of food to appear alert and also so that no one can ask you anything. Look left and right so you appear to still be engaged. (See Emotional Intelligence Plan)

9. Get up and start pacing. For added points, pace behind the person who's talking. This will make everyone nervous. (See Trick #7)

10. Stare out the window with your back to the room, sighing deeply.

11. Leave to take a phone call. (See Trick #9)

12. Return and stand near the door, as if you might leave again at any time.

13. Finally sit down in a different chair, throwing everyone off.

14. Wonder aloud about how the CEO would respond to this conversation. (See Trick #67)

TEAM
MEETINGS

HOW TO MANAGE OPTICS
LIKE A BOSS

Whether it's called a stand-up, status meeting, or all-hands, these time sucks are those inescapable daily, biweekly, weekly, monthly, quarterly, or yearly requirements that never, ever go away, long after everyone's started wondering why it's still on their calendars.

If you can nail looking smart in these meetings, you might be lucky enough to run them someday, at which point you can quit.

#33 Sit next to the person leading the meeting

Sit next to the person leading the meeting. Act as if you are conferring with him about the agenda and backing him up at the appropriate times. This will give the rest of the team the perception that you're co-leading the meeting. And when folks are giving their updates, it will seem like they are presenting their updates to you, as well.

#34 Discuss the process

When someone gives her update, ask if we're really using the right process there. This will likely derail the meeting into a discussion of what the right process is, at which point you can point out that it would be good if our process was clearer. This will make you seem like a strategic, goal-oriented team player.

#35 Interrupt someone's update, then let him finish (The Kanye)

If someone is giving an update on a project, interrupt him and let everyone know how important this update is. Then ask the person to continue. This establishes your dominance over the meeting.

#36 Ask for a time check

How are we doing on time?

Remind everyone to be brief with their updates, because we want to keep this meeting brief. Anytime you try to shorten the meeting you'll seem like a hero, even if it results in longer or more meetings. When you start your update, ask how much time you have. If there's only five minutes left, say you really need six so you'll save your update for next time.

THE MEETING–E-MAIL CYCLE

Source: TheCooperReview.com

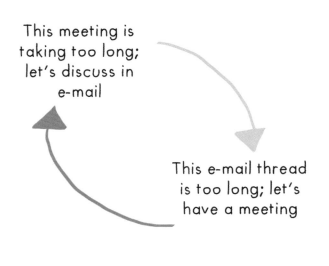

This meeting is taking too long; let's discuss in e-mail

This e-mail thread is too long; let's have a meeting

#37 Use the royal 'we' even when you aren't involved

When discussing someone else's project, always use the royal 'we,' even if you have nothing to do with it. Say things like, 'When do you think we'll be done with that?' 'We should really focus on that,' or 'Wow, we really f*cked that one up, didn't we?'

#38 Remind everyone that we have limited resources

Does everyone already know we have limited resources? Yes. Do you still look smart when you bring it up? Definitely.

#39 When someone asks a question, look at the person who you think has the answer

Often you'll have absolutely no idea what the answer is to any question that's being asked. But that doesn't matter. You can still appear smart by looking around the room to the person everyone else is looking at, who hopefully has the answer to whatever the question is. If no one has the answer, seem really disappointed so everyone knows how much he or she has let you down.

#40 As the meeting is ending, ask a few people to hang back to talk about a separate issue

Margaret, could you stay back a second?

When you ask one or two people to stay a few extra minutes, it makes the rest of the group wonder what you'll be discussing, why they weren't invited, and what top-secret project you've got brewing up your sleeve. They'll assume it's something big, even though you're just seeing if maybe we should have doughnuts next time.

ATTENDING MEETINGS IN A MALE-DOMINATED WORKPLACE

Like most women, I'm not a man. But as a working woman in the working world, I'm surrounded by them. The sausage factory has inundated every industry from government to tech companies to actual sausage factories, so it's imperative that everyone knows you're not there to serve coffee. Here are my 8 favourite tricks for dominating the male-dominated workplace.

1. USE SPORTS METAPHORS

If there's one thing men understand, it's sports metaphors. If someone did a good job, say it was a home run. If you're going to the bathroom, say it's par for the course. Using a sports metaphor is hands down the best way to skate to where the puck's going to be and keep the ball rolling before you throw in the towel.

2. GIVE GOOD HIGH FIVES

You'll be surprised to learn that high-fiving is a cornerstone of male congratulations in the workplace. Giving a good high five is appropriate in almost any situation – nailing that big pitch, free bagels in the break room, washing your hands after you pee. Slam your high five hard to assert your strength. Make sure no one is looking before you wince in pain.

3. LEARN HOW TO TALK ABOUT CARS

The men in your office are all going to talk about cars eventually, so you may as well learn what they know the same way they learned it – by visiting ferrari.com, porsche.com, and lamborghini.com.

4. NEVER MAKE ANY STATEMENT THAT SOUNDS LIKE A QUESTION, EVEN QUESTIONS

Most women sound like they're always asking a question, even when they're not? Don't do that. Make everything you say sound like a forceful statement. Your male counterparts might be intimidated by your confidence and eventually avoid you, but they will certainly respect you.

5. COMPLIMENT HIS SOCKS

Men have only two opportunities in life to express themselves fashion-wise: their left sock and their right sock. So focus on his feet and compliment the hell out of them. Make him feel like the hundreds of hours he wastes picking out socks is totally worth it.

6. WHEN YOU'RE ASKED TO DO SOMETHING BECAUSE 'THEY NEED MORE WOMEN,' LAUGH IT OFF

You might be asked to give a presentation, go to a business dinner, or attend an event specifically because 'they need more women.' Always laugh off this complete insult to your worth as a human being and never make a big deal about it. Save your complaints until you're with your girlfriends and don't cry about it until you're home alone in bed where no one can see your tears.

7. PRANK EARLY, PRANK OFTEN

Cover his pen collection with glitter. Switch his regular coffee with decaf. Leave him a voicemail message in your boss's voice saying that his compensation will be reduced significantly next quarter due to market fluctuations. You may think pranking is harsh or insensitive, but you need to rub that compassion right out of your heart if you're going to fit in.

8. QUOTE *THE BIG LEBOWSKI*

Or *Animal House*. Or *Rudy*. Or *Hoosiers*. Or whatever stupid movie they can't stop talking about.

IMPROMPTU
MEETINGS

HOW TO HANDLE MEETING SNEAK ATTACKS LIKE A NINJA

An impromptu meeting might be disguised as a 'quick question,' 'quick check-in,' or 'quick chat,' but these meeting sneak attacks feel more like 'quick reasons you should have worked from home today.'

The key to appearing smart in an impromptu meeting is to seem excited, available, and open to any discussion while also thwarting any attempt at meaningful conversation. This way, they'll walk away (quickly) thinking you are the smartest person in the hallway.

#41 Openly welcome the meeting

I always have time for you, Steve

Immediately stop what you're doing and ask your colleague how he is. Seem genuinely excited to see him. This will make you seem approachable and transparent. When others describe you, they will use the words 'friendly' and 'warm.' This will distract from any shortcomings you have in knowledge or talent.

#42 Give a compliment

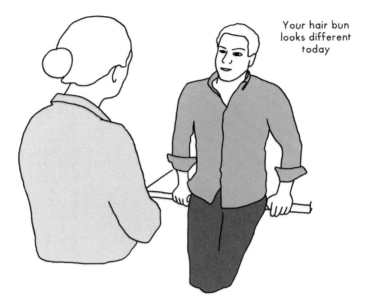

Your hair bun looks different today

Giving a compliment is a great way to seem truly interested in your colleague while also making her feel a little self-conscious and awkward. She'll momentarily forget why she came over to talk to you in the first place, which will make her seem disorganised. By comparison, this will make you seem like you really have your shit together.

#43 Say 'I have to dash in five minutes'

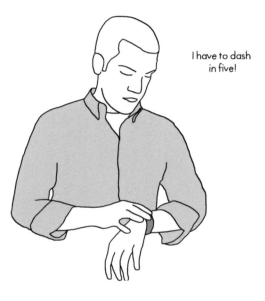

I have to dash in five!

Before your colleague has a chance to begin, let him know that you absolutely cannot talk for more than five minutes. This will make him think that every minute of your day is smartly accounted for. Your colleague will now feel the need to get to the point quickly, and if he can't, he can send you an e-mail instead.

#44 Say 'I just need to make sure I'm not missing anything else right now'

I'm a slave to my calendar, you know

Of course you'd love to talk, but you need to just make sure you're not missing anything else right now. Take your time checking your calendar and e-mail on your laptop. Then check your phone. Then check your tablet. Then go back to your laptop. Then say it looks like you're free, until something comes up.

#45 Pull someone else into the conversation

Pulling someone else into the conversation will give you 'connector' status – and make you seem like you know whom to talk to about what. Once the third person joins, remember that you have another meeting and leave your two colleagues to continue the impromptu meeting without you.

#46 Say you'd love to document this conversation

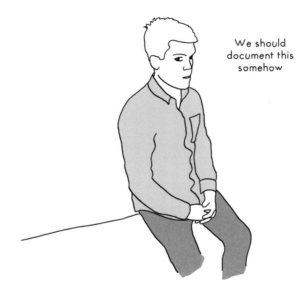

We should document this somehow

If your colleague begins talking in detail about a project, say that an e-mail might be better so that the conversation can be documented. If they say they already sent you an e-mail about it, ask them to send it again because it probably got buried. Then spend five minutes complaining about how many e-mails you get and how so many people are waiting on your input on several different things.

#47 Say you're listening even though you continue to type

Interject with a few uh-huhs and mm-hmms every now and then while you type random words into a document. Your multitasking skills will seem very impressive.

#48 Ask to see the data

Why don't you send me the data?

Pride yourself on 'data-based' decision making and always ask to see the data before the conversation can move forward. If your colleague has the data, ask for more. If she has more, ask her to summarise it. By the time you get the summary, the data will be out of date, so ask for the latest data.

HOW TO MAKE YOUR MEETING SEEM LESS LIKE A MEETING EVEN THOUGH IT'S TOTALLY A MEETING

One way to make meetings less painful is to do whatever you can to trick people into thinking it's not a meeting. Sure, everyone still knows it's a meeting, but this little trick will make people expect something different, productive, even enjoyable.

But Sarah, you say, won't this just lead to an even greater sense of disappointment when the person realises it is, in fact, another meeting? Yes.

Here are three fun tricks for making your meeting seem less like a meeting even though it's totally a meeting.

1. CALL IT SOMETHING ELSE

It's a good idea to avoid using the word 'meeting' when scheduling your meeting. Try calling your meeting by a different name to throw folks off the scent of the fact that it is really a meeting. Here are some fun alternative names for your meeting:

- huddle
- office hours
- stand-up
- powwow
- pulse check
- fun time
- extravaganza
- rally
- forum
- quorum
- summit
- come to Jesus
- brain date
- circle back
- tag up
- check-in
- follow-up
- TGIF
- tea time
- meet-up
- town hall

2. GIVE YOUR CONFERENCE ROOMS FUN NAMES

The practice of giving conference rooms cool names dates back to 1976, when it didn't work then, either. Simply pick a fun theme for your conference rooms and no one will ever realise that this is where their happiness will go to die.

Here are a few conference room themes you can use for your office:

- **Lofty goals you'll never achieve:** Singularity, Time Travel, The Respect of My Father, Revenue
- **Geniuses who are smarter than most of the people you'll ever work with:** Einstein, Plato, Buscemi
- **Team qualities:** Lack of Commitment, Avoidance of Accountability, Inattention to Results
- **A grab bag of tech buzzwords:** Gamechanger, Disruption, Uber for Conference Rooms

3. MAKE UP FUN MEETING RITUALS

Make up fun meeting rituals to force people to have fun. These rules can be how you start the meeting, if you sit or stand, or who has the power in the meeting.

- Start with personal sharing about weekend plans
- Have someone else run the meeting each week
- Give a 'success of the week' award
- Begin with a three-minute meditation session
- Sit on bean bag chairs
- To direct a question at someone, shoot her with a Nerf gun
- Pass around a 'talking stone'
- End with a secret handshake

HOW TO NAIL THE BIG PITCH BY NOT SAYING MUCH OF ANYTHING

The key to any successful presentation is to not make an ass of yourself in front of your colleagues. For some, this means lots of practice and careful preparation. For people who don't feel like doing that, it means following these 12 tricks. These subtle tricks will carefully mask how little you know about that thing you're supposed to be an expert on.

#49 Start with a shocking fact

I never knew my father

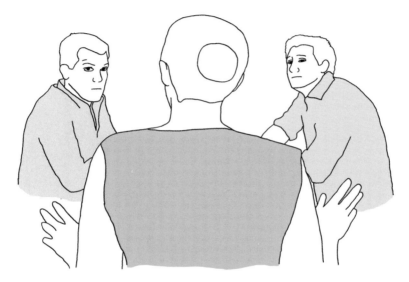

Begin your presentation with something strong and memorable, such as a personal story you stole or a shocking fact that no one is quite sure is true. This will immediately get everyone's attention for a minute or two and then be stuck in their heads for the rest of the presentation so they don't listen to anything else you say.

#50 Hold a pen and a few papers

Make sure you're always holding something, whether it's a pen, a few loose pieces of paper, or both. This makes you seem overly prepared, gives you something to use while pointing, and makes it easy to quickly refer to your 'notes' or pretend to be taking notes.

#5/ Introduce your project by comparing it to other more successful projects

Great Inventions

Wheel   Smartphone   Our latest spreadsheet widget

An easy way to make whatever you're presenting seem incredibly important is to put it at the end of a list of memorably successful things. Talk about the wheel, electricity, the internal combustion engine, the iPhone, or overnight shipping. Then say that the thing you're talking about follows in the footsteps of those incredible inventions, like you truly believe that.

#52 Say you really want this to be interactive

Feel free to interrupt me with thoughts or questions anytime

Allowing your audience to stop you at any point is an effective way to avoid having to give your presentation at all. This is helpful especially when you totally forgot to prepare anything, or procrastinated until the last minute then fell asleep. Ask open-ended questions such as, 'What do you want to hear about?' or more pointed ones such as, 'Jenna, what do you think about our earnings last year?' When people give their responses, lean against the wall and nod, then look around the room and ask, 'Anyone else?'

#53 Put one large word on each slide

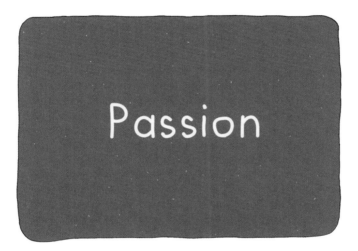

When designing your slides, simply put one large word in the centre of every slide. This word can be in white text over a dark background, in black text over a light background, or in white text over a half-opaque field over a photo you stole from Google Images. Read the word aloud, then look at the audience and say, 'I'm just going to let that sink in.' If they aren't completely overwhelmed by your intelligence, they'll at least be wondering why they aren't.

#54 Ask someone else to control the slides

Yeah, so just open that up and figure out how to project it...

Asking someone else to run the slides for you immediately puts you in a position of power where you can say things like, 'Next slide, please,' 'Just go back a few slides,' and 'Please try and keep up with me, Janet.'

It also gives you leeway to walk around the room, put your hands on your hips, and keep everyone on their toes about where you'll roam next.

#55 Before moving on, ask if it's OK to move on

Is it OK if I move on?
Am I going too fast?
Is everyone OK if
I move on?

There's nothing like a condescending, 'Is it OK for me to move on?' to make your audience feel like a class of year sevens at story time. Ask for a verbal confirmation that it's OK to move on. Make sure to ask this of the whole room but while looking at only one person. Then pause and say, 'Next slide, please.'

#56 Skip over several slides

Oh, yeah, we can skip this slide. Oh, yeah this one, too. Yeah, this one, too, no wait, go back, yeah, skip this one.

Grab several slides from previous presentations or presentations from your colleagues and put them in between the slides you made. Then just skip over these quickly saying, 'Oh, we can skip this for now,' or 'I'll come back to this if we have time.' Your colleagues will think you spent hours and hours over-preparing for your talk.

#57 Say 'That's a great question' before you avoid each question

That's a great question. I'll follow up about that later

Besides being a great way to stall until you can think of a way to avoid the question, complimenting the asker also makes you look like a generous presenter. After you comment on how great the question is, no one will even notice when you say something like, 'You'll see the answer if you just keep listening,' 'Let me address that at the end,' or 'Let's follow up about that offline.'

#58 When a director makes a comment, stop to write it down

If a director or other higher-up makes a comment, immediately stop your presentation to write it down. Say, 'Great point, Sheila, let me just make a note of that,' being sure to call her by her first name (or a nickname) so everyone knows you guys are pals.

#59 Sit on the edge of the table

Sitting on the edge of the conference table will make you seem more informal, without taking away your air of superiority. Try calling someone's name and speaking directly to him. Then look off into the distance like you're deeply contemplating something. Your audience will be mesmerised.

#60 Ask the audience to come up with key takeaways

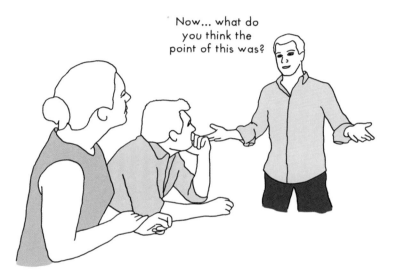

Every good presentation ends with key takeaways, but smart presenters always ask the audience what they thought they were. Don't worry about the initial awkwardness. If the silence becomes deafening, just call on someone and act like whatever she says is total brilliance. Make a note of it.

MEETING-SPEAK CHEAT SHEET

This wasn't on my calendar	=	I deleted this from my calendar
Duly noted	=	I've already forgotten about it
Let's table that	=	That's the dumbest thing I've ever heard
Can you repeat that?	=	I was looking at Facebook
To your earlier point...	=	I'm kissing your ass
That said...	=	We're still not changing anything
Let's streamline this process	=	Let's keep talking about this forever
It's a no-brainer	=	I don't feel like thinking about it

Definitely	=	Probably not
Can I ask a quick question?	=	We are going to be here a while
Happy to discuss this further	=	Don't ever bring this up again
On a related note	=	I'd like to change the subject
Thanks for bringing that up	=	You're going to regret bringing that up
Sounds good to me	=	I have no idea what you're saying
Let's get some data on that	=	I'm pretty sure you're wrong
I'll try my best	=	I'll do the bare minimum
Let's circle back later	=	I need this to be over
I'll set a reminder to follow up on that	=	You will never hear from me or see me again

BRAIN-
STORMING
MEETINGS

HOW TO BE PERCEIVED AS THE CREATIVE FORCE ON YOUR TEAM

In a brainstorming meeting, the pressure of coming up with incredible new ideas can be debilitating. Luckily, the last thing most corporations want is new ideas. During these largely pointless exercises, the point is to contribute using the mere gravitas of your presence, make other people's ideas seem like your ideas, and look like a true leader by questioning the efficiency of the whole process. That's how you kick ass at a brainstorming meeting, and here are 12 tricks to look like you're doing just that.

#61 Leave to get water and ask if anyone needs anything

Anyone need anything? Water? Snacks? Coffee? Tea? Snacks? Tea?

Just before the meeting starts, get up and ask if anyone needs anything. People will think you're so thoughtful, kind, and giving, plus you'll be able to disappear for 10 minutes no questions asked. Even if no one wants anything, return with bottles of water, soda, and snacks. Your colleagues will feel compelled to start drinking and snacking, and your foresight will make them think you can really predict the future.

#62 Grab a pad of sticky notes and start drawing

While the topics are being introduced, grab one of those sticky note pads and start drawing meaningless flowcharts. Your colleagues will look over at you with worried interest, wondering how you're coming up with so many complex ideas even before you know what this meeting is for.

#63 Make an analogy that's so simple it sounds deep

When everyone is trying to define the problem, make an analogy about baking a cake, or something just as completely unrelated. Your colleagues will nod their heads in agreement, even if they really don't understand how what you're saying is related to what they're talking about. Talking completely over their heads will make you seem wildly transcendent and intimidatingly creative, even though the truth is you really just like cake.

#64 Ask if we're asking the right questions

Shouldn't we be asking if this ask is the right ask?

Nothing makes you seem smarter than when you question the questions by asking if they're the right questions. If someone responds by asking you what you think the right questions are, say you just asked one.

#65 Use an idiom

We're polishing a turd

Using an idiom to question an idea is a subtle, smart way of questioning it. Here are some idioms to choose from:
- Isn't that gilding the lily?
- Isn't that putting lipstick on a pig?
- Seems like we're polishing a turd.

#66 Develop a quirky, creative habit that 'gets your juices flowing'

Develop a quirky habit that 'helps you think' and 'gets your creative juices flowing.' This could be anything from showing up in your pyjamas, meditating on the floor, jogging on the spot, throwing a ball against the wall, air drumming with your favourite drumsticks, or all of those things at the same time. Even if you're not actually coming up with any ideas, your colleagues will be intimidated by your uncontrollable creative energy.

HOW TO STRATEGICALLY
SHOOT DOWN SMALL IDEAS

Source: TheCooperReview.com

Wonder if an idea seems too small
so your colleagues see you as a
big thinker and a gamechanger.

Use one of these phrases:

- But how is it disruptive?
- Is this 10x?
- Is this the future?
- I thought that was dead.
- What's the big Win?
- But isn't Apple doing that?

HOW TO STRATEGICALLY SHOOT DOWN BIG IDEAS

Source: TheCooperReview.com

Wonder if an idea seems too big so your superiors see how much you care about company resources.

Use one of these phrases:

- Is it too disruptive?
- How does this fit into the roadmap?
- This seems like a pivot.
- Isn't that a nonstarter?
- Isn't that out of scope?
- But how would you test that?
- Will that work internationally?

#67 Say how you think the CEO would respond

This sounds like something Melissa would really love

Make your colleagues think that you have a very close relationship with the CEO by bringing up how you think she would respond to an idea. Mention your CEO by her first name. Say you might run this by her during your next powwow. Congratulate everyone for coming up with something she'd like. By associating yourself so closely with the CEO, people will start to think of you as some kind of CEO-in-training.

#68 If someone comes up with a good idea, say you had that same idea years ago

It's like you took the words right out of my mouth

If someone comes up with an idea that everyone seems to like, say you had the same idea before. This way you've aligned yourself with the good idea by indirectly taking credit for it.

#69 When an idea has potential, challenge it by playing devil's advocate

When an idea has potential and everyone seems to like it, that's a good time to play devil's advocate. Take an assumption that everyone's making and turn that assumption on its head. Then say you're just playing devil's advocate. Your colleagues will see you're considering the problem more deeply than anyone else and be impressed with your ability to continue talking in circles about this for another three hours.

#70 Ask if we're creating the right framework, platform, or model

We need to be building a platform

You will always appear as if you're thinking bigger than everyone else by bringing up a framework for moving forward, or a model of thinking, or how we can turn this into a platform. It's a very meta way of blowing everyone's minds and masking the fact that you have no idea what everyone's talking about.

#71 When everyone seems to like an idea, yell out 'Ship it!'

Ship it!

There'll come a point when everyone seems to be really excited about an idea or direction. At this point you should try to be the first person to yell out 'Ship it!' Sure, it's a funny thing to say that will make people laugh, but doing this will also convey some authority on your part to both end the meeting and make a final decision, even though you have no power to do either.

#72 Take pictures of the ideas at the end of the meeting

After the meeting is over, stay back and take pictures of the whiteboard, corkboard, chalkboard, and any board that has anything on it. Then e-mail your pictures to the rest of the attendees and thank them for such a fruitful discussion. Then immediately delete the images because you'll never, ever do anything with them. Ever.

PART
THREE

Next Steps

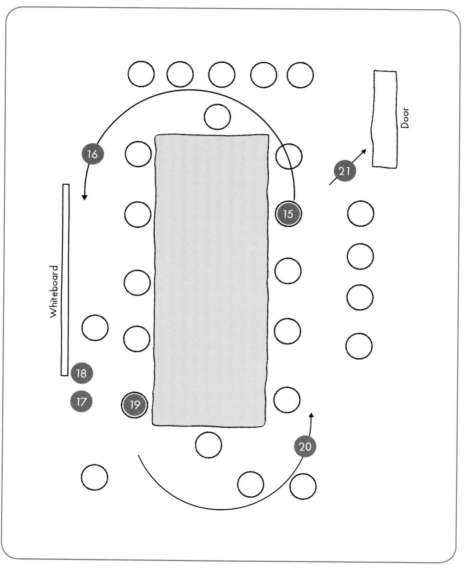

Door

Whiteboard

LEAVING THE ROOM

The final 20 minutes of the meeting is a key time to make sure everyone leaves the room remembering your contributions. Since you didn't make any contributions, though, you'll have to make them think you did by using these final, meeting-winning tricks.

15. Nod vigorously while taking notes in your notebook. (See Trick #4)

16. Write 'roadmap' on the whiteboard, then put a square around it. (See Whiteboard Tactics)

17. Lean against the wall and wonder if we're thinking big enough.

18. Make an analogy about baking a cake. (See Trick #63)

19. When someone asks if we've covered everything, return to your seat and say you had a few more thoughts but you'll follow up later. (See Trick #32)

20. Ask that two people hang back to talk about a separate issue. (See Trick #40)

21. Excuse yourself and leave them on their own.

HOW TO BUILD RELATIONSHIPS WITH PEOPLE YOU'LL NEVER SEE AGAIN

The most important thing to remember at a networking event is not to punch everyone you meet in the face.

Most people hate networking events, but I see them as a great opportunity to appear influential and well-connected to people I've never met and will never meet again. From your name tag to your handshake to pretending to be interested in other people's lives, each part of a networking event is important.

Keep in mind these 10 tricks while you walk around wishing you were anywhere else.

#73 When someone asks what you do, use words like 'proprietary' and 'technology' and 'exciting'

I'm working on a proprietary dog-walking technology; it's very exciting

Spice up any boring oral CV by describing your work as 'proprietary' or appending the word 'technology' to any term. And be sure to say how you're very excited about all the incredibly exciting things you're doing.

#74 Don't wear your name tag

I don't believe in
name tags

You'll always look smart if you don't follow all the rules and appear to be doing things 'your way' (meaning, what I tell you to do in this book). One way to do this is to not put on your name tag. When someone asks you where your name tag is, say you don't believe in name tags and you think people should just talk to each other. People will find it hard not to agree with you.

#75 When someone mentions something you've never heard of, pretend you've heard of it

So you know about real-time updates?

Know about them? I love the stuff

Always nod in agreement when someone starts talking about an app, book, or person you've never heard of. If they ask you about your experience with said app/book/person, say something generic about how you're not sure it's the right platform, or the concept was fuzzy, or you thought she had a great handshake. Then excuse yourself to get another drink and avoid this person for the rest of your life.

#76 Drink when everyone else does

When the person you're talking to drinks, take a drink, too. This is a subtle cue to let people know you're really fitting in. It also ensures that no one expects you to fill the silence.

#77 Say you're here to build your network

I love growing my network

Let people know that you're here to build your network. This makes it clear that you already have a network and you're just here to make your network even bigger than it already is. Use computer sciencey analogies to describe your relationships. Talk about the nodes and connections in your network and how you want to be a bridge between the firewalls of free-flowing knowledge sharing.

WHAT ARE WE DOING
AT NETWORKING EVENTS?

Source: TheCooperReview.com

33% Avoiding everyone

23% Pretending not to be waiting in
line to talk to the important people

85% Asking why it's not an open bar

45% Overcompensating

99% Pretending you read that book

82% Wishing you were home watching
Netflix

90% Hanging just on the outside of a
group of people who are talking
and laughing, wondering what it
must feel like to be accepted

#78 Introduce people as if they should already know each other

When you have the opportunity to introduce two people, make a really big deal about the fact that they didn't know each other before. Say things like 'I can't believe you don't know Devin!' or 'How haven't you met Allison yet?' Your colleagues will feel the inexplicable need to thank you for the introduction and mention to their friends that you introduced them, and worship you like the god of networking you are.

#79 When someone asks for a business card, say you might have one left

Oh, shoot, I might've given them all away

Always make it seem like you might have just given your last business card away but then finally find one. This will make it seem like you've already gotten a lot of important networking done. It will also make the other person think the business card you gave her was your last one, so she might wait a few extra hours before throwing it away.

#80 Ask people to tell you their story

What's your story?

Never ask someone what she does. Ask her to tell you her story instead. If the person answers with what she does, say, 'Sure, that's what you do, but that's not who you are,' and ask her to tell you her story again. This is akin to asking someone a question she'll never know if she's answering correctly, which will make her feel sort of dumb and think you must be much smarter than she is.

#81 If someone asks you what you're working on, say it's pretty confidential

I wish I could say more about it, but you'd need to sign an N.D.A.

Avoid getting into specifics about what you're working on by saying that your project is 'hush-hush,' 'under wraps,' or 'on the down low.' Say you can't say anything more without having them sign a non-disclosure agreement. The more secretive your response, the more powerful you'll seem, and the more the other person will believe you're working on something important, and definitely not spending all day reading Wikipedia articles about dinosaurs.

#82 To get out of a conversation, say you have some people waiting on you

It's never easy getting out of a pointless conversation, let alone getting out of 18 pointless conversations every hour. One great way to do this is to say you have some people waiting for you. The fact that there are people waiting for you is impressive enough, but add to that the fact that you don't want to keep them waiting, and, well, you're bound to be seen as some sort of corporate celebrity. Your colleagues will secretly be wondering who's waiting for you (your Uber driver).

WHAT TO DO
WITH YOUR HANDS
DURING A
NETWORKING EVENT

The number-one area of failure for most people during a networking event is an obvious lack of things to do with their hands. Even if you have the most interesting job title in the world, no one will want to talk to you if your hands are flailing about aimlessly. To avoid this networking event catastrophe, try one of these handy activities.

1. Hold a drink casually with one hand. Then switch to the other hand. Then switch back.

2. When someone asks you how the drinks are, use this hand gesture.

3. Bury your hands in your pockets to add an air of mystery to your marital status.

4. Crossing your arms lets people know that you aren't easily impressed, and also it's chilly in here.

5. Call the waitress to bring hors d'oeuvres and show people you're no stranger to being served.

6. Point and wave at the waiters to make it seem like you're always polite to the staff.

7. Cover your mouth in shock when someone tells you she just moved back in with her parents.

8. Hold up your credit card to let everyone know you're getting some points for these drinks.

9. Holding your jacket makes people wonder why you don't trust coat check.

10. This deeply introspective pose shows people how deeply introspective you are.

11. Clasp your hands behind your back while slowly pacing and silently judging everyone.

12. Thoughtfully adjust your glasses as you listen to someone's business plan.

13. Who's got two thumbs and loves conferences? This guy!

14. Grooming your eyebrows shows you care about your neat appearance.

15. Use this gesture to get someone to repeat the amount of funding his start-up just got.

16. Playfully challenge your drinking partner to a karate match and pretend you know karate.

17. Yawning might be considered rude, but say you're just tired from an all-nighter, not bored out of your mind.

18. Scratch your head when no one thinks it's weird how everyone here has 'Director' in their official titles.

19. When you see someone approaching whom you don't want to talk to, take a large bite of food and then point at your mouth.

20. Let everyone know you're gonna go mingle with a casual thumb over the shoulder.

21. Air drumming shows everyone how musically inclined you like to pretend you are.

JOINING THE
CORPORATE CULTURE CLUB

To appear smart at a teambuilding offsite, you must be prepared for intense pretending on both a physical and mental level. Although most offsites these days don't involve traditional trust falls, you'll likely still have to levitate a copper rod in unison, play an improv game, or otherwise appear to really connect with your team.

This means showing that you've grown and learned something, encouraging others in their learning and growth, and wishing for even more learning and growth in the future.

#83 Wear running gear or yoga pants

Show up wearing your yoga, running, lifting, or tennis outfit. Do some light stretches before the activities start. This will make people think you've exercised in the past year. Bonus: When you get tired after about an hour, your yoga pants are great to nap in.

#84 Say you wish we could do this every day

Seem genuinely excited to be out of the office, even if you're just in a conference room at a hotel and you'd really rather be sleeping under your desk.

#85 Make a vague statement about how this activity relates to what we're facing on our team

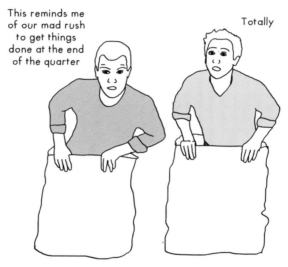

This reminds me of our mad rush to get things done at the end of the quarter

Totally

Playing tug-of-war? Relate this to how you're always fighting internally for the same resources. Setting up a human shield? Say something about how you often feel like your company isn't protecting you. Solving a maths problem? Say how much you hate maths. Relating every mind-numbing exercise back to the team will make you seem deeply abstract.

#86 Wonder how we can incorporate these activities into our staff meeting

I hope we can work these ideas into our daily stand-ups

Make a comment about how fun this is and how everyone is working together so well. Then ask, 'How can we work this into our day-to-day?' Say it's a rhetorical question that you'd like everyone to think about for the future.

#87 Ask for an 'energy check'

How's everyone's energy levels?

After lunch, ask how everyone's energy levels are doing, and say you want to manage everyone's energy. Let everyone know that having good energy is important and if we have low energy, we should really do some kind of energetic exercise.

#88 Cheer randomly

Every once in a while, let out a 'Woo hoo!' or a 'Go team!' or both. Your enthusiasm will make you look like a true team player.

#89 Say how much you genuinely like your colleagues, as if it's a huge revelation

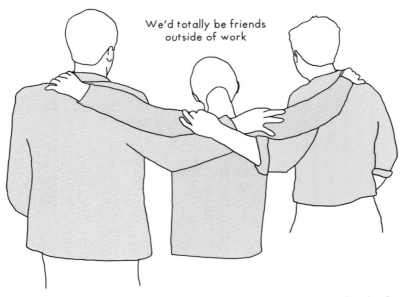

We'd totally be friends outside of work

Pretend to look at your colleagues as if you're seeing them for the first time, before you knew how annoyingly passive-aggressive they would be on a daily basis. Say how much you really like them and how lucky you are to work with people who are so cool. This will make your colleagues feel special, as if you truly care about them.

#90 Ask for a group high five

When the event is over, ask for a team hug or a high five. Then say how impressed you are with how it was organised and ask for a round of applause for the organiser. This will ensure that whoever organised this event gets stuck with the next one, too, so that you don't have to deal with it.

FAMOUS MEETINGS THROUGH HISTORY

What can we learn about meetings from the most famous meetings that have ever taken place? Use these golden nuggets to nudge your team toward success, and your ability to appear smart will transcend time and space.

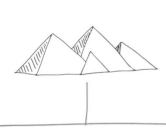

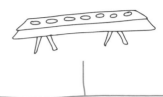

The Pyramids
2630 BC

Can you imagine working a project without being able to track any success metrics until the afterlife? That's what the ancient Egyptians did. Their ability to undertake projects that spanned hundreds of years can teach us a lot about quarterly planning.

The Trojan Horse
1190 BC

When nothing else was working, the Greeks pretended to give up but actually were hiding inside a giant wooden horse. Needless to say, when this idea came up, everyone thought it was crazy — and if it hadn't worked, someone definitely would have lost a job.

The Last Supper
Wednesday, 1 April, 33 AD

You thought you were the only one with a mandatory business dinner on slump day? Jesus was the Managing Director of his time, making sure to get full approval for a lavish dinner from his CEO. Shortly thereafter, he received the highest promotion.

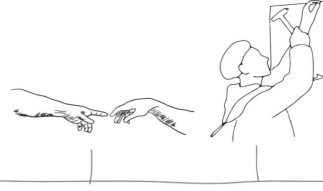

The Knights of the Round Table
450 AD

King Arthur's table was round because everyone had equal power. Silicon Valley is just getting into the holacracy game, but distributed authority existed long ago and their tactical meetings were incredibly efficient, according to legend.

Sistine Chapel
10 May, 1508

It's tough to find good contractors these days, isn't it? And it was tough back in 1508, too. It took seven years to convince Michelangelo to sign on the dotted line, and then it took him 11 years to finish the project. Luckily, he was able to give consistent status updates that kept everyone focused on the big picture.

Martin Luther's 95 Theses
31 October, 1517

As the first known corporate mission statement ever written, Martin Luther's 95 Theses was an early precursor to Brad Garlinghouse's Peanut Butter Manifesto. Martin Luther's fate was no different. In 1521, Luther was condemned at an All Hands Meeting of the Holy Roman Empire. He went into hiding but then triumphantly returned to lead his own successful company, The Lutheran Church.

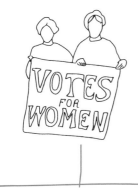

Women's Suffrage in America
1756

Finally, a woman, Lydia Taft, is allowed to vote in the town meeting in Uxbridge, Massachusetts. It was the first victory in colonial America for women in meetings, and now women are encouraged to speak up in meetings around the world, as long as they still smile and agree with everything.

Meeting of the Five Families
1931

The first meeting of the New York Five Families established a rule of consensus among the Mafia and was certainly an earlier predecessor to today's PayPal Mafia. However, the real heroes here were the ones doing the scheduling. Finding an evening where each of these mobsters was free was a logistical nightmare 10 times worse than a dead body floating in the river.

Recording of 'Do They Know it's Christmas'
25 November, 1984

During this famous Band Aid recording, Status Quo rockers Francis Rossi and Rick Parfitt were hungover and weren't able to sing their parts. But they showed up anyway to share bottles of booze and a bag of cocaine, turning the recording into a party. In one afternoon they proved that bringing tea to a meeting can go a long way towards making people think that you actually contributed.

ADVANCED MEETING POWER MOVES TO GET YOU PROMOTED (OR FIRED)

A tiny handful of you have likely already mastered appearing smart in meetings and have been promoted numerous times as a result. This is true for most midcareer executives who've clocked in over 15,000 hours of meeting time. But what about the next 15,000 hours? For that, you'll need to move on to some advanced tactics.

Find some inspiration in these (unverified) stories of unabashed meeting brilliance, successfully executed by the most powerful leaders in the corporate world.

Sorry, guys, I'm going to lose you below 10,000 feet

CONFERENCE CALL WHILE SKYDIVING

In the summer of 2012, a well-known tech executive gave a presentation from a helicopter hovering over the convention centre where his company's keynote was taking place. Then he jumped, putting every other video conference call in history to shame.

LUNCH MEETING EXCEPT YOU'RE
THE ONLY ONE BEING SERVED FOOD

A certain San Francisco executive never attends meetings in the office. Instead, he invites his team to his house overlooking the water, where they meet in his grand dining room. He alone is served lunch by his personal chef, while they present their weekly reports to him and go hungry.

BRING ALONG YOUR MASSEUSE

Another well-known tech executive is known to attend meetings while receiving a massage, saying it helps his 'process of organic decision making.' He arrives with his masseuse, who carries his massage chair, then proceeds to deliver his 'uh-huhs' and 'mm-hmms' while the kinks in his neck are worked out.

SCHEDULE AN INTENSE, MULTIDAY MEETING

What problem can't be solved by sitting together in a conference room all day, every day, for five days straight? Champion this as a great way to tackle the need for big ideas, team dynamics, or product fixes, and get someone else to plan it and run it by promising him a promotion at the end of the quarter (but still take credit for coming up with the idea).

Keep in mind there is a direct correlation between insane meeting behaviour and how smart people think you are. But try these tactics only if there's little to no chance they can fire you (like if you're the CEO or if you're a pretty reliable witness in an ongoing sexual harassment lawsuit).

BUSINESS
DINNERS

HOW TO APPEAR SMART IN FORCED SOCIAL SITUATIONS

If you have a business dinner on your calendar, that means you're well on your way to becoming a very important person. Not only can you now tell your colleagues that you're leaving early to attend a business dinner but also you can tell your family you're not coming home because of a business dinner, and you can say to your Mum, 'Sorry, Mum, I'm at a business dinner.'

Once you're at the business dinner, however, you need to do everything you can to ensure no one realises you probably shouldn't have been invited.

WHAT TO TALK ABOUT
AT A BUSINESS DINNER

Source: TheCooperReview.com

TOPICS TO DISCUSS

Leonard Cohen
Your Mastermind group
Meditation
Night vs. day doulas
Broadway
How to cook duck
The importance of storytelling
Made in Chelsea
Your love for kale
Your triathlon training
SpaceX
Humanitarian missions
The future of technology
Porchetta

TOPICS TO AVOID

Freemasonry
Being an evangelist of
    anything
Your 'experiments'
Your favourite shotgun
Alien conspiracy theories
Your struggles with in vitro
The Only Way is Essex
The career you wish you had
Your teenager's latest arrest
Bodily functions
Bacon

#91 Bring your laptop bag

Always bring your laptop bag to business dinners. Your laptop doesn't actually have to be in the bag; simply having the bag makes you look like you're going to be heading home after dinner to continue working.

#92 Whisper something to the person next to you, then laugh

Mark's fly was down
all day
today

Lean over and say something into the ear of the person next to you –
it can be anything from 'It's kind of cold in here, isn't it?' to 'Where
are the breadsticks?' or 'Do you know when this thing is supposed to
be over?' Whatever you say, it'll make you look like you're discussing
something secretive and important.

#93 Ask the waiter for a recommendation, then order something that isn't on the menu

Asking for advice makes you look smart. Completely ignoring it and leaving everyone wondering why you bothered to ask for anyone's opinion in the first place makes you look like a CEO.

 Order a drink

Depending on what you order to drink, there are several ways to appear smart.

If you order a glass of wine: Ask when the bottle was opened. This makes it seem like quality is very important to you.

If you order a speciality cocktail: Order something exotic that no one's ever heard of; this way you'll seem like a real trailblazer.

If you order beer: Make sure your beer is as dark as your CEO's soul, if that's even possible.

If you order water: Give your waiter a disapproving look if he offers you tap water. (See Emotional Intelligence Plan)

#95 Look your colleague in the eye and say 'Cheers' in a foreign language

Egészségedre!

Remind everyone that it's seven years of bad sex if you don't look each other in the eyes while toasting. It will make you seem like you care about tradition and know history or something. Then learn how to say 'cheers' in some foreign language. This will make you seem worldly, like you really could handle those international accounts.

#96 When someone asks, 'What are you most excited about in the coming quarter?' say, 'Innovation'

I'm excited about innovation

When the topic of what you're most excited about comes up (and it will), talk about innovation. Mention something about innovation efforts and innovation opportunities.

#97 Volunteer someone to give a speech

Volunteer the most senior person at the table to give a speech about the future. If you're the most senior person, volunteer the newest person to talk about what he loves most about his new team.

#98 Tell someone she's made a good point and then pull out your phone to jot it down

Great point, let me write that down... 'espresso baristas...on Mondays...'

When one of your colleagues makes a point about something he seems to think is interesting, pretend to be impressed and say you don't want to forget it. Pull your phone out and make a note of it. This makes you look like you have any power at all to do anything about what he just said. It also gives you a chance to check your messages without appearing rude.

#99 Suggest a seat switch

How about a seat swap?

Long dinner tables force you to have a conversation with the same person all night. Ask for a seat swap to give everyone a chance to mingle; it'll make you look like you care about camaraderie and get you out of having any conversations that are too deep.

#100 Say 'Ping me about that tomorrow'

Why don't you ping me about that tomorrow?

If anyone brings up work-related items, ask him to ping you about it tomorrow. Since the booze is going on the company account, there is literally no way he will remember to actually do it, but you'll seem important in the moment.

And after all, isn't that what really matters?

FOLLOW-UP

IN BETWEEN MEETINGS
DOWNTIME IS
YOUR TIME TO SHINE

Even when you're not in a meeting, it's important that you continue to appear smart.

1. SEND A THANK-YOU E-MAIL
After each meeting, send an e-mail to all attendees and thank them for taking the time to meet. And thank the organiser for organising and thank the note taker for taking notes. And thank the person who brought snacks. And if no one brought snacks, suggest there be snacks next time.

2. WALK AROUND WITH YOUR LAPTOP OPEN
Use an antiglare screen on your laptop so that no one can tell you're actually reading the news.

3. ALWAYS USE A 'SENT FROM MY PHONE' E-MAIL SIGNATURE
Use a 'sent from my phone' signature, even when you're not sending from your phone. This makes you look like you're always busy and on the go and also gets you out of proofreading.

4. SAY YOU DIDN'T SEE THAT ON YOUR CALENDAR

Instead of showing up to a meeting, simply don't. When you are pinged about joining, say you didn't see it on your calendar. The fact that they couldn't start the meeting without you will make you look very important.

5. SUGGEST A MEETING

When an e-mail thread gets past 25 replies, a contest of efficiency has begun and the first person to suggest a meeting is the winner. Be that winner. Suggest that meeting.

6. REQUEST A POSTMORTEM

When a project gets cancelled, request a postmortem to determine what went wrong. Say you'd really like to be there when the postmortem is presented, so you can learn from others' mistakes.

7. COMPLAIN ABOUT HOW MANY MEETINGS YOU HAVE

Always complain about how many meetings you have, but never say exactly how many – just take how many meetings other people have and double it. That's how many meetings you have.

8. WRITE A MEMO ABOUT UNPRODUCTIVE MEETINGS

Send a memo saying how you wish meetings could be more productive.

9. SCHEDULE A MEETING CALLED 'QUICK CHAT' WITH ONE OF YOUR MORE ANNOYING COLLEAGUES

Then keep postponing it at the last minute without any explanation. When he asks what the meeting is about, say you'll discuss it in the meeting, which you know will never happen.

10. SCHEDULE A MEETING ABOUT REDUCING THE NUMBER OF MEETINGS

Get everyone together in a room and wonder if there should be meeting-free days, or meeting-free afternoons, or meeting-free mornings. Run out of time and decide to continue the discussion in another meeting.

Many, many thanks to everyone who read and shared the original article on Medium, Facebook, Twitter, and everywhere else; all of my extended social media family for their continual support, ideas, and feedback; Matt Ellsworth, Tamara Olson, and David Bishop for reading and improving each and every early draft; Christian Baxter, Sophie Gassée, and Jeffrey Palm for being my fearlessly believable meeting models; Ossie Khan, my skydiving expert; the most kick-ass agent and best lunch date in the world, Susan Raihofer (and Christina Harcar for bringing us together); the most patient editor in the world, Patty Rice; the entire team at Andrews McMeel for supporting this project and welcoming me to the family; my sister, Charmaine, for enduring endless text messages; Mom, Dad, Rachael, George, Susie, Ryan, Tyler, Irene the Fourth, Irene the Fifth, and, most of all, my husband Jeff, the person who cracks me up and keeps me going. I love you.

1 3 5 7 9 10 8 6 4 2

Square Peg, an imprint of Vintage,

20 Vauxhall Bridge Road,
London SW1V 2SA

Square Peg is part of the Penguin Random House group of companies
whose addresses can be found at global.penguinrandomhouse.com

100 Tricks to Appear Smart in Meetings copyright © 2016 by Sarah Cooper.

First published by Square Peg 2016

www.vintage-books.co.uk

A CIP catalogue record of this book is available from the British Library

ISBN: 9781910931189

Printed and bound in China by Toppan Leefung Printing Ltd